IMAGES OF ENGLAND

SHROPSHIRE AIRFIELDS

In the early days any large field was a potential airfield and, before the First World War, famous aviators toured the country in their aircraft giving demonstrations. This is Gustav Hamel's Bleriot Monoplane on 18 July 1912 at the Hinstock Show in the grounds of Hinstock Hall. The Number 3 was the aircraft's number in the regular air races which took place at Hendon, where Hamel was something of a star.

A Handley Page O/400 in 1918 at Tern Hill, one of three Shropshire airfields during the First World War. Towards the end of the war it was designated a training station for the formation of heavy bomber squadrons. This O/400 is unusual in that it has Sunbeam Maori engines, made in nearby Wolverhampton. The engines of choice for the O/400 were the Rolls-Royce Eagle and the Liberty, and the lower powered Maori was only fitted when these were not available.

IMAGES OF ENGLAND

SHROPSHIRE AIRFIELDS

ALEC BREW AND BARRY ABRAHAM

The
History
Press

First published in 2000 by Tempus Publishing
Reprinted 2004

Reprinted in 2009 by
The History Press
The Mill, Brimscombe Port,
Stroud, Gloucestershire, GL5 2QG
www.thehistorypress.co.uk

British Library Cataloguing in Publication Data.
A catalogue record for this book is available from the British Library.

ISBN 978 0 7524 1760 8

Typesetting and origination by
Tempus Publishing Limited.
Printed in Great Britain.

Contents

In the Second World War Shropshire came to be littered with new airfields. The most exotic of these was to be Atcham, where the United States established a Combat Crew Replacement Centre. Here is a typical scene with two of the bases' P-47 Thunderbolts, two Harvard trainers and a Noorduyn Norseman communications aircraft.

One of Shropshire's most famous pilots was Flight Lieutenant Eric Lock, DSO, DFC and bar. Born at Bomere Heath, his family later farmed near Condover, and Eric was inspired to take up flying after many hours watching the gliders of the Midland Gliding Club on the Long Mynd. He joined the RAFVR and learned to fly at Meir, near Stoke-on-Trent. During the war, flying Spitfires with No.41 and then No.601 Squadrons, he shot down twenty-five German aircraft. He died on a fighter sweep over France on 3 August 1941.

Introduction

During the late 1930s and the Second World War Shropshire came to be a county covered in airfields, as it was an area designated to hold many of the major training stations the Royal Air Force needed for its great expansion. This had mirrored the example of the First World War, when training airfields were opened at Shawbury, Tern Hill and Monkmoor.

In the days before the First World War, any large field could be pressed into use as an airfield and, from 1911 onwards, a number of famous pilots of the day toured the country giving flying demonstrations at many local communities. None of these fields could really be classed as airfields, though a number of them did later become the sites of airfields.

After the First World War flying ceased at Tern Hill and Shawbury, though it continued to be seen at Monkmoor, near Shrewsbury, for some years. The Berkshire Aviation Company, which toured the country giving joy flights in its small fleet of Avro 504Ks, used Monkmoor's hangars as a base whenever it was in the Midlands in the late 1920s. In 1933 Sir Alan Cobham's Flying Circus also used Monkmoor for one of their National Aviation Day Displays, but the expansion of Shrewsbury largely put an end to flying there. Alan Cobham's Circus returned to Shropshire the following year with dates at Oswestry, Shrewsbury and Bridgnorth, but did not return again until September 1935, when they displayed at Whiston Cross near Cosford.

The only airfield to see regular flying after Monkmoor closed was on the Long Mynd, where the Midland Gliding Club set up base, to exploit the lift generated by the westerly winds which hit the hill. However, things were to change with a vengeance as RAF expansion got underway.

In the late 1930s a major new airfield for the training of ground-based trades was established at Cosford and new flying training airfields were built at the former airfield sites at Shawbury and Tern Hill. Three large maintenance units were established in these three airfields for the storage and preparation of aircraft for RAF service: No.9 at Cosford, No.24 at Tern Hill and No.27 at Shawbury.

The storage of aircraft on these three sites expanded to such a degree during the war years that dispersed sites were used and a number of Satellite Landing Grounds (SLGs) were also brought into use. These SLGs were usually just grass airfields with few buildings to house a minimal staff and often utilized the grounds of a nearby stately home to store aircraft. Such SLGs existed at Brockton, Hodnet, Weston Park, and Ollerton. The latter was destined for a rather more glamourous role, as it was eventually handed over to the Fleet Air Arm, which needed an airfield in central England for blind-flying training. Ollerton was expanded, given a mesh runway, and eventually renamed Hinstock, or HMS Godwit to the Navy.

A further very large MU, No.29, was established at a substantial new airfield built at High Ercall, which was also used by night-fighter squadrons covering the north west and later became a major night fighter Operational Training Union (OTU).

The two major training airfields, Shawbury and Tern Hill, had purely grass surfaces and, as the pressure on them built up, bad weather caused severe problems. The long-term answer was to provide paved runways, but in the meantime a number of Relief Landing Grounds (RLGs) came into use, often little more than a large grass field, with the minimum of permanent buildings. Different units used at different times Bratton, Bridleway Gate, Child's Ercall and Chetwynd, as well as other satellites outside the county.

Child's Ercall was developed during the Second World War as a major flying training station in its own right, eventually being renamed Peplow and serving as a bomber OTU. Further major training airfields were built on new sites within the county. Two fighter training bases were built at Atcham, opening in September 1941, with a satellite airfield at Condover, and Rednal, opening in April 1942, with a satellite at Montford Bridge.

Atcham was to achieve further fame when it was handed over to the United States Army Air Force, to establish a Combat Crew Replacement Centre to train American fighter pilots in British weather conditions before posting them to operational squadrons.

Another bomber OTU was established at Tilstock, on Whitchurch Heath. This large airfield also had a satellite built at Sleap.

At the end of the war the run-down of most of these airfields was rapid. The only stations with a long-term life were the three major pre-war training airfields, at Cosford, Shawbury and Tern Hill – with satellite airfields at Sleap and Chetwynd – and the large storage airfield at High Ercall. The latter was to close in the early 1960s but the others have continued in use to the present day.

Cosford's future is assured as the only training station for ground-based trades in the RAF and, though Shawbury's future was in the balance for a while, it eventually triumphed over Middle Wallop in Hampshire as the home of the tri-service helicopter training school. Tern Hill is only used as a satellite airfield for Shawbury, with the Army taking over the accommodation, but Sleap has found a new use as the home of the Shropshire Aero Club and the general aviation airfield for central Shropshire.

Flying has resumed on many of the former RAF airfields, as private individuals operate from part of Peplow and Rednal and a Parachute School uses part of Tilstock. The microlight movement has even seen the opening of new airfields at Market Drayton and Shifnal. Perhaps the most surprising survivor is Chetwynd, one of only two grass airfields still regularly used by the RAF, the other being Weston-on-the-Green, which has rather more in the way of facilities than little Chetwynd. Meanwhile, up on the Long Mynd, the gliders and sailplanes of the Midland Gliding Club continue to soar and swoop over the Shropshire hills as if the noisier comings and goings on the Shropshire Plain had never happened.

A Spitfire of No.61 Operational Training Unit at RAF Rednal, near Oswestry, in 1942. No.61 OTU operated Spitfires at Rednal from April 1942 to the end of the war, using RAF Montford Bridge as a satellite airfield.

One

RAF Atcham

Atcham was built as a standard RAF fighter sector station to accommodate two squadrons, with its satellite station being Condover. The first squadron to arrive was No.131, which arrived with the first of its Spitfires on 27 September 1941. These were replaced by No.350 (Belgian) Squadron in February 1942, which shared the airfield with No.74 Squadron for about two months, before the latter went to the Middle East and No.350 moved to Warmwell. In April 1942 No.232 Squadron reformed at Atcham with its Spitfires, but a month later moved to Valley. The Luftwaffe were no longer penetrating so far into north-west England and Atcham was handed over to the United States Army Air Force.

For the rest of its life the airfield served as a training centre for American fighter pilots trained in the clear blue skies of America, getting them used to British weather conditions and working them up to operational status. The first unit to arrive was the 31st Fighter Group, which was supplied by the RAF with fifty Spitfire Vs and began training in June 1942. The 31st left at the end of July and was replaced by the 14th FG which flew its Lockheed Lightnings across the Atlantic.

When the Lightnings moved on, the first of the P-47 Thunderbolts began to arrive and equipped the 551st and 552nd fighter squadrons, making up the 495th Fighter Training Group, which was to provide all the P-47 replacements pilots for the 8th and 9th Air Forces. Later, in August 1944, eighteen P-38 Lightnings were also added to the Group's strength as the unit began providing P-38 replacements as well.

The Americans left Atcham in February 1945 and the airfield became a satellite for No.5 (P) AFU at Tern Hill for a while, before flying ceased completely in April 1946.

A special Republic P-47-2-RE Thunderbolt with a lengthened fuselage and a water-injection system for the engine. This was the personal mount of Atcham's base commander Major Ervin Miller, who used its superior performance to impress his pupils in mock dog-fights. At the time it was the only P-47 in Great Britain in a natural metal finish.

American Bell P-39 Aircobras gathered at Atcham in July 1942 before being despatched to North Africa.

Atcham's control tower with American jeeps and personnel outside. The tails of an RAF Spitfire and a Lockheed Lightning are visible to the right. Both these types served at Atcham before the Thunderbolts arrived.

The Headquarters building at Atcham with a motorbike outside. The Stars and Stripes is at half-mast which suggests a recent accident. There were many during the Second World War, as pilots trained in clear blue American skies came to terms with British weather conditions. This building still stands as part of the Atcham Industrial Estate.

P-47s being maintained on the external hardstandings. There were three large Callender Hamilton hangars at Atcham plus seven small blister hangars, like the one visible in the background.

The entire permanent Army Air Force staff at Atcham, or Station 342, as the Americans numbered it, on 14 June 1944. They came from thirty-two different states of the Union, plus the District of Columbia. There are also three RAF officers, Sqd. Ldr Wooding (from Northampton) is sixth from the right, front row; Sqd. Ldr Leighton (from Montford Bridge) is third from the right, front row, and Fl. Lt Essem (from Gillingham) fifth from the right, third row. Major Miller is ninth from the right, the front row.

A P-47 Thunderbolt, having come to grief in a watery location somewhere in Shropshire.

Another P-47 Thunderbolt, having made a wheels-up forced landing in a wheatfield. There were 137 accidents during the war at Atcham, involving thirty-seven fatalities.

A front view of the control tower at Atcham with the airfield code 'AP' outside.

Major Miller's office in the control tower, with the Assistant Operations Officer, Captain Kis, at his desk in the corner.

A group outside the control tower just before Major Miller took his wife on a flight around the Wrekin in a Piper Cub. From left right: the on-duty Controller, Major Ervin Miller, Mrs Miller, Captain Kis. Chock-to-chock races around the Wrekin relieved the monotony for the instructors later in the war.

The 495th Fighter Training Group buildings.

Major Miller and Captain McKinney, the Engineering Officer, with the 495th Fighting Training Group maintenance and engineering crew in front of one of their charges.

The Motor Pool at Atcham. The number of surviving buildings at Atcham has steadily declined over the years, as they have been replaced on the Atcham Industrial Estate with more modern buildings.

The students reading room in the 495th Group buildings.

The Officers Club bar with two snooker tables, rather than the more familiar pool tables.

The Mess Hall on a special occasion, judging by the flowers on the tables.

Two

RAF Bridgnorth

There was never an airfield at RAF Bridgnorth but, as so many Royal Air Force personnel passed through its gates, mostly for their initial training, it's hard to ignore it. As it was often their first taste of service life, the base has left an indelible impression on many former RAF personnel. Also there were usually aircraft to be found in the Camp, acting as gate guardians, or inspirations to the new recruits.

The camp is actually at Stanmore, three miles from Bridgnorth, but there was already RAF Stanmore in Middlesex so, when it opened in November 1939, it was called RAF Bridgnorth. It was built as a temporary camp, No.4 Recruit Centre, where new recruits were given their basic training. Later in the war, more specialized training took place at Bridgnorth, with No.1 Elementary Air Navigation School established, followed by the School of Flying Control and a battle training course.

Initial training, however, remained the Camp's main purpose and this continued after the war. The end of National Service caused a contraction of the armed services and RAF Bridgnorth was one of the casualties. The Station closed on 7 February 1963 and became an industrial estate.

A picture taken just inside the main gate of RAF Bridgnorth in the 1950s. The Hurricane IIc on the left is LF686, while, just visible on the right, is a Vampire F.3, VT801.

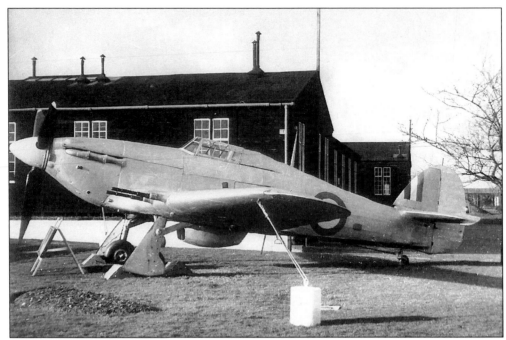

A close up of perhaps the most famous of the Station's 'gate guardians', the Hurricane LF686. It is now preserved in the Air & Space Museum, Washington D.C., after the RAF Museum swopped it for the world's last Hawker Typhoon.

Within the Camp was Gloster Meteor F.3, EE405, which had the Maintenance Serial 5897M.

A group of squaddies gathered around the stove in their hut, c.1959. They are making tea and toast, a popular pastime.

A group of squaddies gathered in front of a Spitfire within the Camp. This is probably the Mark Vc, BM597, which was later used to make the mould for the plastic Spitfires in the 'Battle of Britain' film, and has since been restored to flying condition as G-MKVC.

No.23 Flight, outside the drill hangar at the back of the Camp in 1956. The hangars still remain, although they have been modified for industrial use.

A Wolverhampton Corporation bus passes through the Camp on a snowy day. It was from such a bus that most squaddies had their last view of RAF Bridgnorth as they passed on to pastures new.

Three

RAF Cosford

With the expansion of the Royal Air Force in the late 1930s, RAF Cosford was built as the No.2 Technical Training School, to augment No.1 School at Halton. It was built by a local company, Sir Alfred MacAlpine & Sons, and included accommodation for No.9 Maintenance Unit as well as the school.

The first arrivals actually came from Halton in July 1938, as one wing of apprentices transferred. During the war over 70,000 airframe and engine fitters and armourers were trained at Cosford, which was also the home of one of three centres for the training of Engineering Officers.

No.9 MU, with aircraft delivered by No.12 Ferry Pilot Pool, stored so many aircraft they took on Satellite Landing Grounds at Weston Park and Brockton. The shadow factory at Castle Bromwich also used some hangars near the railway station for the assembly of Spitfires, which were flight-tested on the airfield.

Cosford's technical training role has continued after the war and it has now become the sole centre for the instruction of ground based trades. Nevertheless, for many years Cosford was far more famous as the home of British Indoor Athletics, with a permanent indoor track in one of the four large workshop buildings. More recently it has become almost as famous for its Aerospace Museum which has steadily increased in size and stature, reflected in its new name of the RAF Museum, Cosford.

A typical flying scene at Cosford for much of its life, as gliding has dominated the flying from the small airfield. On a hazy sunny morning around 1960, a group of Air Training Corps cadets gather around a Slingsby T.31B glider.

In August 1939 strange shapes started appearing in the countryside between Albrighton and Shifnal. Concrete Type E storage hangars began to spring up, ready to house the aircraft in store with No.9 MU.

On the other side of the airfield from the curved Type E storage hangars, a row of Type D hangars were built to house the instructional airframes of No.2 School of Technical Training as well as more of No.9 MU's charges.

On the other side of the railway from the airfield, this huge accommodation block, known as Fulton Block, was built. It was named after Captain John Fulton of the Royal Engineers, one of the founding fathers of the Royal Flying Corps.

A large camp of officers and airmen's housing was built on either side of the A41 to house the permanent staff at Cosford.

A Type E hangar nears completion, almost ready to receive its covering of turf. They were designed to cast no shadow and attachments for camouflage netting were incorporated to hide each end, which would have made them almost invisible from the air.

A group of engineering students receive instruction in propeller swinging on the airfield in 1940, surrounding a camouflaged de Havilland Gipsy Moth, probably an impressed civil machine. In the background are two Hawker Harts, one without wings.

A Boulton Paul Type D gun turret fitted to the tail of a Handley Page Halifax in February 1944. The two 0.5in. Browning machine guns and the AGLT scanner (radar) have not yet been fitted to this experimental turret, which was to equip Lincolns after the war.

An Avro Lincoln under the care of No.9 Maintenance Unit, just after the war. There is still a Lincoln at Cosford, on display in the RAF Museum, and said to be haunted.

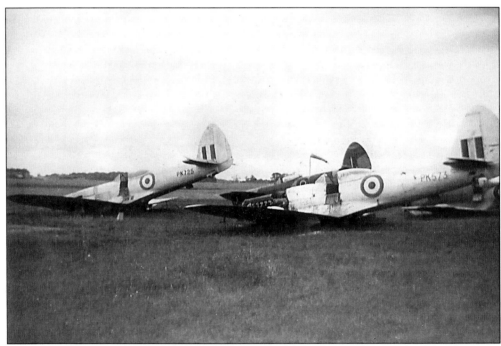

A group of Griffon-engined Spitfire Mk.22s and 24s awaiting the smelter at Cosford in the mid-1950s. They are on the Albrighton side of the airfield. A sad sight, they are a reminder that the Castle Bromwich Shadow Factory operated a Spitfire assembly unit during the Second World War, in the Bellman hangars by the railway station.

An Air Training Corps Slingsby T.21 two-seat glider coming in to land on the grass at Cosford, c.1959.

A group of ATC cadets gathered round a Slingsby T.21 c.1959. Note the use of a Land Rover to keep the wing down!

A Slingsby T.31B Cadet TX.3 coming in to land on the grass at Cosford. The T.31B was developed from the Slingsby Motor Tutor, which itself was produced by fitting a new fuselage with an engine to the single-seat Cadet TX.2.

One of the Gloster Javelins used as an instructional airframe at Cosford during the 1960s, inside one of the Type D hangars. These hangars are usually full of recently retired RAF jets.

A stranger in town: an Army Air Corps de Havilland Beaver taking part in the annual air show at Cosford in the mid-1960s. A Shackleton is flying in the background.

An Army Westland Sioux helicopter flies over a Miles Hawk Major during the 1965 Battle of Britain Air Display.

For many years the name Cosford was most famous as the home of British indoor athletics, housed in one of the four huge indoor workshops on the opposite side of the railway from the airfield. This is the cover of the programme for an international meeting in 1968, featuring Ralph Banthorpe, a well-known local sprinter.

The Control Tower is one of the few remaining still in use for air traffic control. It was built to the 1959/34 design of brick and, unlike others erected at this time, has remained unaltereted in its appearence. Behind is the C-type MU erection hangar and, further away, the concrete D-type hangar used for short-term storage. Station identity letters in the signal square, 1997.

A visiting air-sea rescue helicopter, Westland Wessex, XV730 in front of Cosford's control tower.

One of the more unusual instructional airframes at Cosford, a Fleet Air Arm Sea Vixen FAW.2, XJ607 (with another Sea Vixen behind) at Cosford in 1986.

Since the war Cosford has always housed a number of historic aircraft and this collection eventually became the Aerospace Museum, now the RAF Museum, Cosford. Here employees from Dowty Boulton Paul Ltd, the local aircraft company, present examples of the company's Power Control Units and a VC.10 model to Derek Eastwood, Museum Curator, (fourth from left).

Prince Bernhard of the Netherlands visiting RAF Cosford in 1980, talking to Group Captain Campbell, the Station Commander.

The Duke of Gloucester (second left) visiting the Aerospace Museum in 1981. He is looking at the Moon Buggy then on display, with Derek Eastwood (third from left).

An Argentinian Pucara aircraft, captured in the Falklands, on display in the Aerospace Museum. This damaged example has since been replaced with another Pucara, which, at the time, was being test-flown at Boscombe Down. Cosford has always displayed examples of 'enemy' aircraft.

The annual air show at Cosford has always been a big local attraction. Here an impressive line-up of participants have made the journey from Duxford. From left to right: Blenheim, Lightning, Mustang, Corsair.

A P-47 Thunderbolt from the Aerospace Museum gets an airing during the Air Show. In the colours of the RAF in Burma, it was a reminder of the Thunderbolts based at Atcham, a little further along the A5, but has now been transferred to Hendon, carrying the spurious serial KL216.

The main display hangar at Cosford in the early 1990s with the Junkers Ju.52 in the British Airways Collection prominent. The Vickers Viking, G-AGRU in the background to the left has since moved to the Brooklands Museum. (*RAF Museum at Cosford*).

A Gloster Javelin faces a Short Belfast and a British Airways Boeing 707 in the Aerospace Museum's outside aircraft park. Amazingly, the 707 was landed on Cosford's relatively short runway, but has recently been scrapped, along with most of the other airliners in the British Airways Collection.

Looking for all the world like a collection of a model aircraft, these are actually real aircraft representing many of the types flown by No.60 Squadron Royal Air Force over the years. They were gathered at Cosford and include a number of the museum aircraft, plus the Blenheim, of the Aircraft Restoration Company, two replica SE.5As and the current equipment of No.60 Squadron, a Bell Griffin HT.1, from RAF Shawbury. (*RAF Museum at Cosford*).

The Type E hangars are still used for aircraft storage! Here a number of gliders share the space with furniture storage.

Four

RAF Rednal

Built in an out-of-the-way place in the depths of north-west Shropshire, Rednal was opened in April 1942 as a standard fighter OTU, with a satellite airfield at Montford Bridge, near Shrewsbury. No.61 OTU was the sole user of the airfield, with its Spitfires and Miles Masters.

The Spitfires were mostly used examples, in the early days including ex-Battle of Britain aircraft. Not surprisingly, with young pilots, old aircraft and adjacent hills, the accident rate was high. The nearness of Atcham and its Thunderbolts naturally caused many mock dog-fights, which could not have helped the accident rate.

Toward the end of the war the OTU also received some Mustang IIIs and the Masters were replaced by Harvards. One morning in February 1945, a German Prisoner of War, who had escaped from a camp near Oswestry, was found sitting in the cockpit of one of the Mustangs, at one of the more remote dispersals. He was apprehended before he could start the engine and gave up without a fight.

In June 1945, No.61 OTU moved out and the airfield was soon reduced to a care and maintenance basis, eventually being sold in 1962. Many buildings are now in use as two industrial estates, with the ones behind the derelict control tower largely given over to a timber company. A small modern hangar holds light aircraft which use part of one of the old runways.

A Spitfire of No.61 OTU ready to go, sometime between the end of 1942 and early 1943. It is at a dispersal at Rednal with trolley-ack connected ready to start-up and a fuel bowser alongside, presumably having just filled it up.

A Spitfire at dispersal at Rednal, with an 'erk' leaning into the cockpit. The 'KR' code belonged to No.61 OTU, which also had a 'shadow' squadron number, No.561, so that in an emergency, it could be immediately turned into an operational squadron.

Accidents were many at most training stations and this Spitfire, wearing the 'TO' codes more normally worn by No.61 OTU's Masters and Harvards, has suffered an undercarriage collapse.

The large Type 518/40 control tower at Rednal with two personnel relaxing on the balcony, c.1944. Note the well-kept garden in front of the tower. The lower floor housed the Watch Office and the Meteorological Office, while the upper floor housed the Aerodrome Control Office. There was also access to the roof.

The Aerodrome Control Staff on the side of the balcony of Rednal Tower in 1944.

A view across the airfield today from the railway bridge over the line which passed closed by. Rednal was so isolated during the war that special arrangements had to be made with the railway to provide trains to Rednal Halt for airmen going on leave or for a night out in Shrewsbury.

The Control Tower today, derelict and backed by a forest of trees in which many of the former RAF buildings are used by a timber company. A new small hangar houses aircraft which use part of the old airfield.

Five

RAF High Ercall

One of the largest airfields in Shropshire, High Ercall had the advantage of being built with three paved runways, thereby escaping the adverse effects of wet weather experienced by Shawbury, Tern Hill and Cosford. It was built as the home of No.29 MU and so featured extensive hangarage on dispersed sites. High Ercall was also unusual because it was a Shropshire airfield with an operational status, housing night-fighter squadrons there to protect the North West. The first was No.68 with its Blenheims, then No.256 Squadron's Beaufighters and the Havocs and Hurricanes of No.1456 Turbinlite Flight.

United States Army Air Corps Squadrons were also resident for a while, the 309th with Spitfires, then the 27th with Lockheed Lightnings, and the 92nd with Bell Aircobras. Other RAF day-fighter squadrons used High Ercall as a station for rest away from the main air fighting. The night-fighter connection was cemented with the arrival of No.60 OTU, training Mosquito night-fighter crews.

After the war, No.29 MU was the main user of the airfield, though its excellent runways were often convenient alternatives for other flying units in Shropshire. The MU closed in February 1962 and the airfield reverted to a care and maintenance basis, before being sold off for agriculture, with the main buildings being taken over by MOTEC, the motor industry training organization. For a while a small hut on one of the dispersed sites on a lane to High Ercall village was turned into a museum by the Warplane Aircraft Recovery Group.

The main entrance to RAF High Ercall, as it looked in 1997, but largely unchanged from the wartime years. The Warden's Office is to the right. This now serves as the entrance to the Centrex (ex-MOTEC) training establishment.

Warrant Officer Sid Walker (wearing a trilby hat!) at the controls of *Doris the Dominie* in January 1943. Sid was a No.456 Squadron Defiant/Beaufighter pilot on six months posting to No.3 Aircraft Delivery Flight at High Ercall. The *Dominie*, X7331, was on charge at No.3 Aircraft Delivery Flight, one of the aircraft used to return pilots back to base. It had previously been named *Hoof-hearted*, but the Station Commander objected and so it became *Doris*.

A page from Sid Walker's log book for February 1943 showing the varied nature of a ferry pilot's life, either retrieving pilots from all over the country in *Doris* or the resident Airspeed Oxford, or delivering assorted aircraft.

Date	Aircraft Type	No.	Pilot	Duty / Remarks
				TOTALS BROUGHT FORWARD
FEB 8	DOMINIE	X.7331	SELF	6 PASS. — BASE - REDHILL - BASE
FEB 9	DOMINIE	X.7931	SELF	6 PASS. — LOCAL (AIR TEST)
FEB 10	DOMINIE	X.7931	SELF	1 PASS. — BRADWELL BAY - SYWELL
FEB 11	DOMINIE	X.7331	SELF	1 PASS. — SYWELL - BASE
FEB 11	OXFORD	AS.894	SELF	5 PASS. — BASE - HAWARDEN - WOODVALE - BASE
FEB 11	OXFORD	AS.899	SGT BENNETT	DUAL INSTRUCTION
FEB 13	OXFORD	AS.899	SELF	3 PASS. — BASE - WOODVALE - BASE
FEB 14	MASTER III	8853	SELF	L.A. KEENAN — HENLOW - CRANFIELD - WHITNEY - BASE
FEB 16	MASTER III	8853	SELF	BASE - WHITCHURCH - BASE — AIR TEST
FEB 17	BLENHEIM	K.7113	SELF	BASE - EGLINGTON
FEB 18	BLENHEIM	K.7113	SELF	BALLYHALBERT - VALLEY
FEB 21	DOMINIE	X.7931	SELF	VALLEY - GRANTHAM. AIR TEST
FEB 24	OXFORD	AS.899	SELF	2 PASS. — BASE - HONILEY - DESFORD - BASE
FEB 26	SPITFIRE	854	SELF	ATCHAM (RETURNED MACHINE u/s.)
FEB 27	OXFORD	AS.899	SELF	4 PASS. — BASE - BALLYHALBERT - BASE
FEB 28	SPITFIRE	854	SELF	ATCHAM. LOCAL (u/s. again)

SUMMARY for 1st - 28th February 1943

UNIT - 3 DELIVERY FT.

DATE: 28.2.43

SIGNATURE: S. Walker

Aircraft Types:
1. DOMINIE
2. OXFORD
3. BLENHEIM
4. SPITFIRE
5. MASTER

GRAND TOTAL (Cols. (1) to (10)] 527 Hrs. 45 Mins.

TOTALS CARRIED FORWARD

Two pilots and two observers in front of the radar-equipped Bristol Beaufighter X7842, of No.68 Squadron at High Ercall between April 1941 and May 1942. The aircraft was named 'Birmingham Civil Defence' having been paid for by the Birmingham ARP.

A Bristol Beaufighter at High Ercall after suffering an undercarriage collapse. The date of the picture is unknown.

Two NCOs of the American 309th Pursuit squadron at High Ercall in June 1942. Part of the first influx of US Army Air Corps personnel, they were accommodated for a while at High Ercall with their Spitfires, before moving to Westhampnett in Sussex on 4 August 1942.

Flying Officer Dennis Moore, Observer (on the left) and Flying Officer John Ayre, Pilot (on the right) at High Ercall in September 1944. They are in front of a No.60 OTU Mosquito VI. This night-fighter OTU had formed in May 1942 at High Ercall. Moore and Ayres went on to complete twenty-six operations.

A Percival Prentice, G-AOPV, at High Ercall in 1956. Most RAF Prentices had been bought by Aviation Traders Ltd for conversion to civil machines, and many of them were parked around the airfield, awaiting transfer to Southend or Stansted.

Some more of the Prentices, including G-AOPS. Most of them were eventually scrapped. At the time High Ercall was only occasionally used as a satellite of Shawbury, and to house 29 MU.

One of the K Type hangars at High Ercall. This one is currently used as a Training Hall for the Centrex training establishment.

An L-Type storage hangar, currently used as a warehouse. Built to store aircraft for No.29 MU, it was originally turf-covered and the hooks for the camouflage netting which could be used to conceal the ends can be seen on the roof.

Not Johnny Johnson with his Spitfire, but Keith Jones of Cannock with his full-scale fibre glass model Spitfire at High Ercall in 1998. With the cockpit fully fitted out with original instruments, Keith continues to add further original parts when he can.

Keith and his Spitfire FSM were part of a small aircraft museum set up at this warden's office on a High Ercall dispersed site by the Warplane Aircraft Recovery Group, which displayed many of the artefacts they had dug up from various Shropshire crash sites. The museum has now moved to Sleap.

Six

RAF Hinstock (HMS Godwit)

The airfield at Hinstock began life as an RAF airfield, designated No.21 Satellite Landing ground, attached to No.37 MU at Burtonwood, and called Ollerton after the nearest village. Because it remained waterlogged after its first occupation in October 1941, it was destined to take on its role as an aircraft storage unit only for a short while, but as a satellite of No.27 MU at Shawbury. It so happened that the Admiralty were looking for an inland airfield on which to establish a blind-flying school. Ollerton was transferred to them on 23 June 1942 and renamed Hinstock, possibly to avoid confusion with Tollerton in Nottinghamshire.

A single wire mesh runway was built, and a perimeter track and additional buildings and hangars were added. The Airspeed Oxfords of No.758 Squadron Naval Instrument Flying School arrived in August 1942. The Lorenz Beam-Approach system was used to teach blind take-offs, flights and landings on a bearing of 217 degrees on Hinstock's single runway. This squadron remained in residence until April 1946, when it was disbanded and replaced by No. 780 Squadron with Oxfords and Harvards. However, when the nearby RAF airfield at Peplow, with its three tarmac runways, became vacant the Navy jumped ship and moved there and Hinstock reverted to agriculture.

Gustav Hamel taxies out in his Bleriot Monoplane at Hinstock Show in July 1912. As the large crowd peering over the hedge testifies, aircraft were a very rare sight at the time and a major attraction for any event with a field large enough to accommodate one. There were 8,000 people at that year's show! The show took place in the grounds of Hinstock Hall. A few days before Hamel had displayed at Wolverhampton and then went to Derby.

'E'Flight of No.758 Squadron in front of one of their Airspeed Oxfords early in 1944.

One of the Airspeed Oxfords, PG983, used for blind-flying training at Hinstock, coded 'UIHH'. There were normally forty in use, with eighteen more held in reserve. This was quite a high number for an airfield with a single runway, which is why Bratton was used as a satellite, when not waterlogged.

One of a small number of de Havilland Tiger Moths also based at Hinstock, mostly for blind spin recovery training. The CO, Captain John Pugh, once hit a concrete picket post while taking off in a Tiger Moth and knocked a wheel off. The duty staff rushed out with a spare wheel and waved it aloft to warn him as he made his approach. He eventually landed successfully.

Three naval lieutenants serving on a 'ship' about as far from the sea as you can get in England, in the depths of Shropshire. From left to right: Ron Smith, Bill Stevenson, Sub. Lt. Stephenson.

The entire permanent staff of officers of HMS Godwit early in 1944. Among them are a number of WRENS including one nurse.

This hut is thought to have been built as a mess hut for the civilian staff employed at Ollerton SLG before the aerodrome was taken over by the Admiralty Still there in April 1982.

Hinstock Hall which was used as the Officers Mess. The owner, Squire Williams, retreated to one wing, but retained the library and the billiard room. The naval officers started a riding club and he allowed them to ride in the grounds. Definitely better than serving on an escort carrier in the North Atlantic!

Three of the officers behind the Mess. From left to right: Bob Long, Ron Smith and Dave Hodgson.

A Stinson Reliant communications aircraft in front of one of the Pentad hangars on Hinstock.

Another communications aircraft, a Beech 17 Staggerwing, also at Hinstock.

The Maintenance Flight at HMS Godwit in 1944 in front of one of their charges. George Preece is second from the right. As he lived in Bridgnorth, he was able to cycle home when he went on leave!

One of the Oxfords on the airfield. Like all blind-flying aircraft, they were painted with a yellow warning triangle to warn all other aircraft to stay well clear. This was very appropriate in the crowded skies of Shropshire, especially as Hinstock's circuit often overlapped with that of Peplow.

Some of the buildings at Hinstock, including a Pentad hangar, in a photograph taken in 1961. One of the hangars now houses Retro Aviation, a dealer in vintage aircraft.

Looking forlorn and unwanted, the unusual three-storey naval type control tower at Hinstock photographed in 1982; one of many such silent sentinels spread across the fields of Shropshire. This building did not come into use until the spring of 1945. Before that a single-storey watch office next to Ollerton Lane was used. This control tower has now been converted into a very luxurious private dwelling.

Seven

Long Mynd

The Midland Gliding Club, which had begun life at a field in Handsworth, Birmingham, using primary training gliders, migrated to the Long Mynd in the late 1930s. A grassy airfield was created on top of the Mynd, with a small hangar and clubhouse and a bunkhouse attached.

The attraction of the hill top site was the lift generated by the hill, especially when the predominate westerly winds were blowing. In such conditions a glider of moderate performance can be kept aloft indefinitely by even a novice pilot. Part of a glider pilot's Silver C badge involves staying aloft for more than five hours; this is far easier to achieve on the Mynd, rather than a flat site, where suitable thermals are required, together with the skill to use them. Pilots often visit the Mynd just to achieve this feat.

Two methods of launching gliders are normally used on the Mynd, either by a winch sited at the far end of the airfield, (the Midland Gliding Club pioneered the second winch method, for retrieving the tow rope), or by bungee launch. When the wind is westerly and in excess of 25 knots, it is possible to launch gliders with a Y-ßshaped elastic rope. Six fit people run down the steep hillside to stretch the bungee, which then launches the glider straight off the hillside.

An Olympia 4 sailplane soaring over the Long Mynd, c.1938. The far end of the Mynd is now covered with a forest, not even planted when this photograph was taken. During the Second World War furrows were ploughed across the landing area to prevent German aicraft using it.

Club members and visitors look up at a glider above the Mynd on 4 June 1936. The glider is flying along the hill using the lift generated by westerly winds.

The famous aviatrix Amy Johnson, on the left, while visiting the Mynd in 1938. Alongside her is the wife of the Club's Chairman, Mrs Espin Hardwick. By this time Amy Johnson had become an accomplished glider pilot and gave demonstrations all over the country.

A Slingsby Falcon glider having come to grief on the Long Mynd on 19 June 1939. It landed short of the airfield near the Cartway, and overturned with little damage resulting. The group of lads who have stopped to watch had just cycled from Wolverhampton. Patrick O'Kane, who took the picture, became an RAF pilot during the war.

A dismantled K.13 after being recovered from a landing fifteen miles away. The pilot entered a 'wave' over the hill and shot up to nearly 10,000ft. The lift was so strong that, when they saw a hole in the 10/10ths cloud which developed below them, they needed to deploy the spoilers to make the glider descend. They emerged well to the west of the Mynd and landed in a farmer's field.

A Slingsby T.43 Skylark awating its turn for a bungee launch to the west. With a west wind in excess of 25mph, gliders can be launched with a Y-shaped elastic rope, with three 'volunteers' on the end of each arm of the Y, who, on a given signal, run down the hill to the west.

Two Schliecher K-13s await the start of the day's gliding. The K-13 flew for the first time in 1966. Developed from the earlier Ka-7, it quickly became a very popular training glider and many hundreds have been built.

The Midland Gliding Club runs weekly gliding holidays, with acommodation in the bunkhouse and unlimited instructions, weather permitting. This is one such course in 1969, all being pupils except the two instructors, sixth and fifteenth from the left. One of the co-authors of this book, Alec Brew, is seventh from the left.

In more recent years the Midland Gliding Club has added a third method of launching gliders to its armoury, the aero-tow. This fomer agricultural spray aircraft, Piper Pawnee, G-CMGC, is currently used.

A German Second World War glider, a Govier 2, being bungee-launched in the 1970s. This side by side two-seater, was used by the Hitler Youth during the war and further examples were built in Holland after the war.

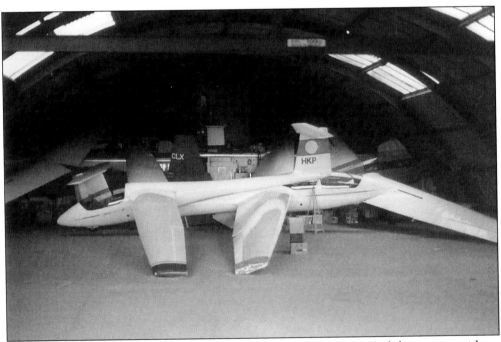

The single-blister hangar can be packed with quite a number of gliders, even without dismantling them, as can be seen in this recent photograph.

Eight

RAF Peplow
(Child's Ercall)

Peplow began life in 1941 as a small grass Relief Landing Ground, known as Child's Ercall, for the Miles Masters of No.5 (P) AFU from Tern Hill. It was then transferred for use by the Airspeed Oxfords of No.11 SFTS, Shawbury, but they complained it was too small. The airfield was then completely rebuilt with three paved runways and renamed Peplow, to serve as a bomber OTU, with No.83 OTU's Wellingtons. However, because it lacked a satellite airfield, it was a so-called $\frac{3}{4}$ OTU.

As D-Day approached, Peplow became a glider towing airfield, with No.23 Heavy Glider Conversion Unit with Albermarle tugs and Horsa gliders. At the end of the war the RAF left Peplow and the Navy, close neighbours at Hinstock, quickly took their place, greatly appreciating the three runways and extra space they had been able to see from their previous base. The station finally closed in 1949 and reverted to agriculture.

It began a new life as an airfield in the 1980s when Dave Williams of the nearby Sambrook Service Station bought part of it to operate his Saab Safir. Using a small blister hangar and a section of the perimeter track on the eastern side as a runway, he doubled his fleet of aircraft with the addition of a Beagle Airedale.

A Hawker Hurricane II, LF380, coded FI-D of the Bomber Defence Training Flight at Peplow in October 1944. The OTU possessed Hurricanes for fighter affiliation exercises with its Wellingtons' gunners, or practice attacks.

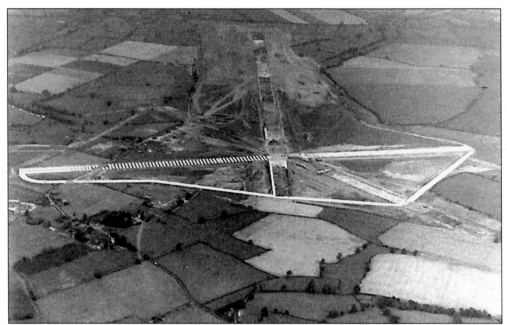

An aerial view of the airfield being entirely rebuilt in August 1942. Previously an all-grass airfield, it was given three main runways, including one especially long one, 04/22, of 2,000 yards, which can clearly be seen, The secondary runway of 1,400 yards, 12/30, is also evident, but the north-south runway, 00/18, of similar length is still being excavated.

When the RAF moved out of Peplow in 1945, the Navy moved in from Hinstock, which was only a mile to the north. No.780 Squadron flew Oxfords and Harvards, including this one coded U2Y.

Surviving buildings on the Technical and Training site in 1961. The large building at the rear was the AML Bombing Teacher. The hangar type building to the left was for vehicles and not aircraft.

The Bombing Teacher still survives today, though now without a roof. During the war there was a real bomb-aimer position inside the building, while below was a moving map, simulating the passage of a target beneath the aircraft.

Dave Williams (right) with his Saab Safir G-BCFW (ex-PH-RLZ) which he keeps in a blister hangar on Peplow, flying from a section of the perimeter track, as the runways have now been dug up. He is with visiting pilots Jim Clarke (Tipsy Nipper from Syford) on the left, and Glen James (Yak from Tern Hill).

A piece of cake! Dave Williams flies his Safir under the bridge on the Hinstock by-pass (before it opened). He is also a regular competitor in air races in his Safir.

Dave Williams also owns this Beagle Airedale, G-AVKP, shown in the mid-1990s, with his blister hangar in the background. The wind sock pole has suffered a little from gale force winds.

A heavily-modified Taylor Titch, G-CAPT, owned by Vic Davies and shown outside the blister hangar.

A visiting Streak microlight, G-MEOW, at Peplow in the mid-1990s.

A visiting Belgian Saab Safir, OO-VOS, at Peplow c.1990. Dave Williams is on the left. Saab owners are a close-knit group.

Nine

RAF Shawbury

Flying training started at Shawbury during 1917 using a variety of aircraft, and the early type Belfast truss hangars were built alongside the western boundary. Everything closed down in 1920 and the buildings were cleared away, although the camp site was used as a repatriation centre until 1922.

Expansion of the RAF led to Shawbury being selected again as a Flying Training School, together with an aircraft storage unit No.27 MU, the first civilian-manned Maintenance Unit. No.11 Flying Training School moved here in 1938, initially with a variety of Hawker biplanes and Avro Tutors, increasingly replaced by Airspeed Oxfords.

Additional airfields across Shropshire were used as satellites of Shawbury throughout the war to ease the burden on the home station, especially when it was still a grass airfield. By the end of 1943 the school, now known as No.11 (Pilot) Advanced Flying Unit, with more than 140 aircraft on strength, moved to Calveley. This was to make room for the Central Navigation School from Cranage which was too small for the increasing numbers of aircraft the unit was operating.

Shawbury was to become the 'home' of navigation, taking on the additional task of Aircraft Control in 1950. The scope of the school changed in 1963 when the navigation element was transferred to Manby and the school was renamed the Central Air Traffic Control School, with Sleap used as a satellite.

In 1976 it was decided to transfer No.2 (Advanced) Flying Training School from nearby Tern Hill. This school remained on site until a change of policy brought the new tri-service Defence Helicopter Flying School in 1997 to take over the work of No.2 FTS and to incorporate Navy and Army helicopter training. The Central Air Traffic Control School became a ground-based unit and continues in this role. Shawbury's main runway also provides a sanctuary for aircraft in an area of the country largely devoid of such facilities.

Station sign board outside the main gates. The station badge was changed to that depicted in 1987 to incorporate three golden lion-heads from the coat of arms of Shrewsbury. The station received the Freedom of Shrewsbury in 1968, with the right to march through the town 'Swords drawn, bayonets fixed, colours flying, drums beating and bands playing'.

The staff of the Officers Mess at Shawbury on 29 March 1919. The station was closed the following year.

The first building of the new Shawbury Airfield being constructed on Shawbury Farm in 1936, as the expansion of the Royal Air Force began to get underway.

The following text appears handwritten on the aerial photograph:

NO. 8 PHOTO
SECRET

COURSE OF BOMBER: 170°
TIME: 0055. DATE: 27/6/40
HEIGHT: ABOUT 10,000'
HALF MOON. SKY CLEAR
NIGHT FLYING ON.
FLARE PATH LIT.
FLOOD LIGHT ON!
WIND FROM 170°
NO WARNING!
7 BOMBS.
NO CASUALTIES!

SHAWBURY VILLAGE

The path of a bombing attack on Shawbury taken on 27 June 1940. A few days earlier during night flying practice, there had been an air-raid warning, with aircraft of No.11 SFTS recalled and the flare-path put out. Night flying then resumed and a Luftwaffe bomber spotted the flare path and dropped a stick of bombs, causing a small amount of damage but no casualties. The fall of the bombs is marked and numbered across this aerial view.

Hard-surfaced runways being built in 1942 to ease the constant pressure on the grass surface. Lines have been painted across the airfield to simulate field boundaries so that it could not easily be seen from the air.

A Short Stirling and crew of the Central Navigation School at Shawbury in August 1944. They had just returned from a navigation exercise flight to Jan Mayern Island.

An Avro Anson T.21, WJ548, of the Central Navigation & Control School, at Shawbury in the early 1950s.

A Percival Provost, XF690, at Shawbury in the 1960s. These aircraft were used by the CNCS and also Central Air Traffic Control School (CATCS) to train air traffic controllers.

A Vickers Varsity of CNCS during a Royal Observer Corps open day. Shrewsbury was the base of No.16 Group Royal Observer Corps (ROC) and the station commander permitted a number of similar days when other ROC groups were invited to attend.

A line-up of Vampire T.11s, used by CATCS, in front of No.1 hangar.

Jet Provost T.4s which re-equipped CATcS after the Vampire T.11s. In the background can be seen a B1 hangar, erected during the war for glider storage and later used to house recoverable items from aircraft which had been scrapped.

Gate guardian Vampire T.11 XD382 was placed in position in May 1969 for the Central Air Traffic Control School, until 1989 when the policy of 'one gate, one guardian' was instituted.

The scrap area at Shawbury in 1964, with a line of Gloster Javelins awaiting the torch.

The scrap area in 1964 held a line of Vampire T.11s, including WZ592, behind an Avro Anson, WB450.

The scrap area in 1960 featured a number of Percival Provosts including XF875. At the time this corner of Shawbury was regularly visited by local aviation enthusiasts to see what it held.

An Anson VP509, being scrapped in 1967, with a Hastings behind. This Anson had served with No.3 Group Communications Flight at Mildenhall. It is recorded as being sold for scrap in 1957, so it lingered on for many years!

A couple of Shackleton MR.2s, including WR957, in front of the Hastings, taken in the same year by a different enthusiast.

A line of Chipmunks of No.8 Air Experience Flight, at Shawbury in 1965. They include WG362 and WZ867. The Flight was re-equipped with Bulldogs in 1995.

Two Handley Page Hastings in store at Shawbury in 1968. They were eventually scrapped on the airfield.

One of a number of Blackburn Beverlies, XM109, in external store in 1968. Along with the Hastings, they were soon scrapped, victims of Britain's withdrawal from East of Suez.

A line of Provosts on the apron at Shawbury in the 1960s.

A selection of aircraft used at Shawbury in the early 1960s: Whirlwind, Provost and Meteor T.7.

Vampire T.11 of CATCS on the apron at Shawbury in the early 1960s.

A Blackburn Beverley visiting Shawbury again in the early 1960s.

A Chipmunk of No.8 AEF landing on runway 01 during 1981. The new runway extension and improved approach lights are clearly visible.

A Vickers Wellington taken at a ROC Cluster Meeting at Shawbury in the 1950s.

This is the original 'control tower' built when No.11 FTS arrived from Wittering in 1938. It housed the offices of the Chief Flying Instructor, flying staff of the school and the Watch Office. Later, full control of all flying movements was carried out. However, by the early 1950s, better facilities were needed and a new control tower was built.

The New Air Traffic Control Building was situated away from the hangar area and placed for a better view of the main runway, given its extension in a southerly direction.

Wessex XS677 had been in service with No.2 FTS until the type was withdrawn. It was then placed in storage for possible sale. The hangar is of Lamella construction, and the diamond shape of the curved roof can clearly be seen. To control temperature and humidity the turf-covering of these hangars was removed and the roof material was upgraded and ventilation units installed.

One of the few Canberras retained by the RAF, WJ866, a T.4, in a photograph taken in 1999.

Hawk XX173 from No.4 FTS Valley in an L-Type storage hangar externally similar to the earlier Lamella, but of different construction.

As Hawks need major servicing this is carried out at St Athan. Airframes are transported by road to Shawbury for storage. The wartime practice of taping over the serial of such aircraft still persists! The hangar used for reception of these aircraft was built of concrete and used at one time by Rootes Securities for assembling and test flying Bristol Blenheims, built at the shadow factories at Speke and Meir.

A number of civilian aircraft are permitted to be based at Shawbury. This Cessna 310, G-MIWS can be seen next to the badge of No.60 Squadron, painted on the door.

Gazelles in storage in a L Type hangar in 1999. The CU marked tails were those aircraft formerly operated at Culdrose by the Navy, the others by 2 FTS at Shawbury.

Squirrel ZJ265 of the civilian operated Defence Helicopter Flying School. Squirrels operate in two squadrons, No.660 of the Army Air Corps and No.705, Royal Navy, though aircraft are not allocated exclusively to either. The large hangar behind is a C Type.

Ex-Fleet Air Arm Wessex XM927 in use with the Fire Fighting Section for training. An L Type hangar of F Site is in the background

Squirrels of the Defence Helicopter Flying School on the apron.

The multi-engined advanced flying training is provided by No.60 Squadron RAF with the Bell Griffin HT.1. Some of the aircraft carried civil registrations for a period: this is G-BXIR. They subsequently acquired military serials and this Griffin became ZJ240.

The very last landing undertaken by a Handley Page Victor on RAF Shawbury's main runaway on 30 November 1993. The aircraft was on its way to the RAF Museum at Cosford but was not allowed to land on Cosford's short runaway for safety reasons. It was therefore landed at Shawbury, dismantled and moved by road. (*RAF Museum at Cosford*).

Gate Guardian Whirlwind HC.10, XP351 'Z' representing the type used by No.2 FTS at Shawbury in 1976-1977. It replaced a Sycamore on the gate in 1988.

An aerial view of Shawbury taken during the early 1970s following final development of the airfield, including an extension to the main runway (a major road had to be diverted) and the V Bomber dispersals. Wartime heavy bomber storage dispersals were still in use and held a number of Armstrong Whitworth Argosies, awaiting scrapping. Alongside the hangar on the extreme left is a Comet C.2.

Ten

RAF Sleap

Situated about two miles south west of Wem, this airfield is well off the main road and reached down narrow roads which were originally airfield-access roads. The airfield opened in the spring of 1943 as a satellite of No.81 Bomber OTU at Tilstock, with Whitleys. Later, when No.1665 Heavy Conversion Unit came to Tilstock, it was decided to base 81 OTU at Sleap, now transferred to Airborne Forces for glider-towing training with Whitleys towing Horsas, replaced by the Wellington for transport crew training in January 1944.

After the war, Sleap's short life as an airfield apparently came to an end when it was put on a care and maintenance basis. Then it had a new lease of life in 1958 when it was refurbished as a satellite for nearby Shawbury, training air traffic controllers, with a GCA caravan sited on the airfield. The RAF finally gave up Sleap in 1964, but yet again the airfield revived as it became the home of the Shropshire Aero Club, operating initially from a hut and the single surviving blister hangar.

Several new small hangars have slowly sprung up alongside this blister and the centre of operations has migrated to the refurbished control tower. A number of friendly air displays and fly-ins have been held over the years on what is a quiet and welcoming airfield.

The Warplane Aircraft Recovery Group have moved into half of the adjacent wooden huts and have set up a delightful small aircraft museum which features mainly artefacts from their crash site investigations, but also displays Keith Jones' Spitfire FSM and a full scale model of a Hawker Fury biplane which normally resides in the blister hangar.

An aerial view of Sleap under construction in August 1942, looking south. The runways are well underway, but much of the perimeter track and dispersals remain to be built and the airfield did not open for another four months.

Miles Messenger G-AKVZ at Sleap in June 1957, with the control tower in its original form in the background. It had been hit by a Whitley bomber during the war, and repaired, which may explain the small windows mentioned on p. 96. Behind the Messenger is an RAF radar truck. Sleap was used at the time for Ground Controlled Approach training, for Ansons and Chipmunks from nearby Shawbury.

Keith Seddon, a radar fitter, in the door of a Bendix MPN1A GCA truck, one of two in use at the time. All RAF personnel stayed at Shawbury, and were transported to Sleap by coach. The aircraft practices approaches but did not at the time touch down. During Keith Seddon's time at Sleap the only aircraft to actually land were a Vampire, which had engine trouble and a Chipmunk, which had an airsick passenger.

An Auster 5D, formerly TJ672, having a wheel change at Sleap during the late 1960s.

A Fairchild Argus, G-AJPI, at Sleap in the late 1960s, with a Slingsby Prefect glider lurking in the background.

Wassmer factory-built Jodel D.120 Paris-Nice G-AXNJ, very often seen within its purpose-built hangar. It was normally a homebuilt type, and this one was imported into the United Kingdom in the early 1960s.

The Sleap control tower is of the conventional type for bomber satellite stations. The lower floor windows have been modified with smaller frames, though the old sills can still be seen. The Shropshire Aero Club now operate the building and it is they who added the observation structure on the roof and the corrugated sheets to the side.

Piper Cherokee Warrior, G-BBXW, once based at Sleap but sold to a new owner in Holland in 1995. It is parked next to the Handcraft hut, used as a store.

Luscombe Silvaire G-BRHY in one of the new small hangars clustered together in one corner of the airfield.

Cessna 152 G-BHAD of the Shropshire Aero Club, used for instructional flying, shown in 1987.

Piper J3C Cub, G-AGVV, a 'period' registration allotted when the aircraft was first imported in 1981 and shown at Sleap during the following year.

An Oldfield Baby Lakes, G-BKHD, imported into the United Kingdom in the early 1980s and based at Sleap for many years. It is shown in a hangar, having work done on the engine, in 1992. Note the track used to push it into the hangar. It crashed near Sleap in 1995 but is now being rebuilt.

Cessna 340 G-BLLY, at Sleap in 1987.

A civil De Havilland Chipmunk, WG472, bringing a flavour of 1950s Sleap, shown there in 2008. The airfield was refurbished in 1958, and RAF landings would have been far more numerous than the early 50s.

A far more exotic resident at Sleap during 2008, was this YAK-3U fighter, D-FYGJ. Built new by the Yakolev company in Russia, who had kept the original jigs since the war, it had been fitted with an Allison engine, rather than the original Klimov.

Eleven

RAF Tern Hill

Tern Hill began life as a Royal Flying Corps airfield during the First World War. It became established late in 1916 as a training station equipped with Avro 504s and later on Sopwith Camels. The flying units were designated as four Squadrons, Nos30, 33, 34 and 43 but just prior to the formation of the Royal Air Force, Tern Hill was designated Training Depot Squadron No.13.

The airfield was allocated to the working up of the new force of Handley Page O/400 bombers but suffered a calamitous fire in March 1919 which destroyed two of the main hangars and many of the buildings on the station, as well as four O/400s and several Avro 504s. The station never really recovered from this disaster and in 1920 was sold to a race-horse trainer.

With the expansion of the RAF in the mid-1930s Tern Hill was a natural site to choose for a new airfield, but such was the infestation of rabbits which had destroyed the surface of the old field, that it had to be completely excavated and relaid. No.10 Flying Training School became operational in 1936, equipped with Avro Tutors, Hawker Harts and Audaxes, and Gloster Gauntlets, which were largely replaced with Ansons and Oxfords as the Second World War approached.

On 16 October 1940 a Junkers Ju.88 bombed Tern Hill and hit the most easterly of the main hangars, destroying the roof as well as eight Ansons and two Blenheims that were inside. The roof was never repaired, although the hangar was still used. It became known as 'The Sunshine Hangar' and was eventually demolished after the war.

Just after the raid No.10 FTS moved to Canada and was replaced by the Miles Master of No.5 (Pilots) Advanced Flying Unit. No.24 MU occupied a group of hangars on the south side, which operated as a separate unit, RAF Stoke Heath. No.5 (P) AFU was replaced by No.9 (P) AFU in 1945 and this was replaced by No.6 Flying Training School in 1946. No.6 FTS remained until 1961, when it was replaced by the Helicopters of the Central Flying School, but these too moved on to Shawbury in 1976, though Tern Hill is still used as a satellite airfield. The accommodation units have been taken over by the Army and house, incongruously, the Staffordshire Regiment.

A Handley Page O/400 heavy bomber at Tern Hill in 1918. At the time it was intended that Tern Hill would be used to work heavy bomber squadrons up to operational status. The aircraft in the background appears to be an RE.7.

AIR LEAGUE OF THE BRITISH EMPIRE

EMPIRE AIR DAY
MAY 23rd   1936

No. 10 Flying Training School,
R.A.F., TERN HILL, Shropshire

In aid of Royal Air Force Benevolent Fund

3d.

Wilding & Son, Ltd., Shrewsbury.

The cover of the programme for the Empire Air Day at RAF Tern Hill, 23 May 1937. The station had been open for less than a year. The photograph features Hawker Harts of No.10 FTS. Hawker Biplanes represented the bulk of the School's equipment.

A Hawker Audax, K747?, on the grass at Tern Hill in 1937. The row of new C Type hangars is behind.

A Gloster Gauntlet fighter, K52??, at Tern Hill in 1937. Unusually at the time, advanced trainers and fighters like the Gauntlet were used by the same School.

An Avro Anson I, K8723, of No.10 FTS which suffered a landing accident at Tern Hill in 1939.

A Hawker Henley target tug, L3244, at Tern Hill late in 1938. This aircraft served with the Central Flying School at the time.

A Douglas Havoc I equipped with a Turbinlite at Tern Hill on 17 May 1942. It was serving with No.1456 Flight (later No.535 Squadron), usually based at High Ercall.

An interesting row of aircraft at Tern Hill on 12 May 1942. In the foreground is the Handley Page 'Sparrow' (a Harrow converted to a pure transport), named *Boadicea*, of No.271 Squadron as K6987. Beyond is an Oxford I, DF255 of No.286 Squadron. Beyond that is Turbinlite Havoc and, in the background, two Hurricanes which appear to be all-black and are therefore possibly also with No.1456 Flight.

A Percival Provost coded 'P-Y' at Tern Hill in 1956, when No.6 Flying Training School was equipped with Provosts.

An oblique picture of the apron taken in 1976. The control tower was greatly modified after the war, from the original Watch Office/Chief Instructors Offices. The hangar behind is a pre-war C Type, but the one in the background is a cheaper version, built later on. The 'sunshine hangar', damaged by a bombing raid in 1940, was to the right.

106

Auster T.7 WE600, on static display at Tern Hill on Battle of Britain Day. This aircraft had been used by the Trans-Antarctic Expedition and is now on display at the RAF Museum, Cosford.

A Saunders-Roe Skeeter XM564, showing the badge of the Central Flying School, which took it over from the Army Air Corps. It later returned to the Army.

Another Provost of No.6 FTS, WV605, at a Battle of Britain Display in 1962. It is now preserved at the Norfolk and Suffolk Aircraft Museum at Bungay.

A De Havilland Devon, VP972, which was a communications aircraft with the Royal Radar Establishment at Pershore, a visitor to the 1962 display.

A Vickers Varsity, WJ910, of No.1 Air Navigation School as part of the 1962 static display. It served at Shawbury, although Tern Hill did have a small number of Varsities on charge at the time.

De Havilland Chipmunk, WK591. Chipmunks were one of the most common aircraft in Shropshire skies during the 1950s and 1960s and even 1970s. This aircraft was demobbed in 1976 and sold in America.

North American Harvard, KF183, which served as a chase plane at Boscombe Down. As a visitor to the 1962 display, it was a reminder of the days when Harvards operated from Tern Hill.

De Havilland Beaver serial 26137, of the USAF, as part of the 1962 static display.

Agusta-Bell Sioux XT138, serving at Tern Hill with the Central Flying School.

Bristol Sycamore HC.14, XG515, coded S-F (The S for Sycamore) formed part of the equipment at Tern Hill in 1966 with its owner 'The Central Flying School' marked on the aircraft. The brick building to the rear of the aircraft was the hangar annexe to the 'sunshine hangar', destroyed by German bombing in 1940.

A Jet Provost of the CFS aerobatic team, the Red Pelicans, at Tern Hill in 1967. The Bellman hangar in the background may have been erected to replace the 'sunshine hangar' and was used for ROC meetings during the 1960s.

Westland Whirlwind HAR.10, XP300, coded W-S (W for Whirlwind) at Tern Hill in1967. This type formed the main equipment of the CFS Helicopter Wing for many years. The CFS badge is by the sliding door.

Gloster Meteor T.7 WH166 was normally based with the CFS at Little Rissington, but is seen here while visiting Tern Hill for the static display in1966. The board on the control tower which says '23' denotes the runway in use, a magnetic bearing.

Blackburn Beverley C.1, XB290. This aircraft was at Tern Hill to give the Royal Observer Corps members meeting at Tern Hill, an air experience flight. It was quite a sight to see this aircraft loaded with ninety ROC members doing a low fly past across a small airfield.

Westland Whirlwind HAR.10, XP355, at Tern Hill, showing its new camouflage paint scheme, though it had bright orange Day-Glo markings and the CFS badge was retained.

The main entrance to RAF Stoke Heath, the 24 MU site, which was quite a separate station to Tern Hill. Seen here behind the typical gates of an RAF Station is the Station Headquarters building now in use as offices, and also the C Type hangar used for aircraft dismantling or assembly prior to storage or repair. The radio mast is an almost unique survivor and was probably used to test radio equipment repaired here in the 1950s.

Twelve

RAF Tilstock

RAF Tilstock began life on 1 August 1942 as RAF Whitchurch Heath but was renamed in 1943 to avoid confusion with Whitchurch near Bristol. No.81 OTU of Bomber Command moved in during September 1942 from Ashbourne. Runways and dispersals were constructed from the start, as well as a number of T2 hangars. A B1 hangar was erected at a later date to house Horsa gliders. Sleap was used as a satellite aerodrome, and the OTU operated Armstrong Whitworth Whitleys.

A bombing range at Fenns Moss some way to the west was used for bombing practice. At the beginning of 1944 the OTU concentrated itself at Sleap and Tilstock became the home of No.1665 Heavy Conversion Unit, with Halifaxes and Stirlings for the Airborne Forces of No.38 Group. Glider towing was practised with Airspeed Horsas on strength.

In March 1945, No.1665 HCU moved out and was replaced by No.42 OTU from Ashbourne to form No. 1380 (Transport) conversion unit with some fifty Wellingtons, spread between Sleap and Tilstock. In 1946 the unit disbanded and the airfield closed, though the hangars were used for the storage of equipment. The main A41 Newport-to-Whitchurch road was reinstated across the airfield and plans were made to extract gravel.

Part of the south side of the airfield was converted into a civil landing strip, on which a Parachute Club flourishes, despite the sign over the door which says: 'Don't take life too seriously, it isn't permanent!'

No.1665 HCU had four Hurricanes to teach the aspiring transport pilots fighter tactics. This one carries the codes of the unit, but its serial is unknown. It is parked outside the sB1 hangar alongside the Shrewsbury to Whitchurch Road.

Fighter Affiliation Flight Chief Instructor R.R. Glass with F/O Baker and three WAAF ground crew with one of the Hurricanes of the Flight.

A Short Stirling towing a Horsa glider, probably southwards on the main runway in 1944. Occasionally aircraft overshot the runway and ended up on the road.

A Horsa coming in to land on a typical steep approach with barn-door flaps deployed. It is under the control of the control pilot in the cupola on top of the black and white chequered van positioned alongside the runway in use.

Tilstock's control tower in 1962, already derelict, with no window glass. It is of the 343/43 type with smaller lower windows, and is bigger than the control tower at Sleap. The window frames have now gone too.

Cessna Super Skywagon, G-DISC, used by the parachute club at Tilstock, though shown here at Tilstock's former satellite at Sleap. It was imported in 1979 and registered G-BGWR, but acquired its new letters in 1984. It has now reverted to the original ones.

Thirteen

Other Airfields

Flying first came to the county of Shropshire before the First World War with the itinerant pilots, like Benny Hucks or Gustav Hamel, who gave flying displays at any convenient field. None of these fields could really be called airfields, though some were to become the sites of just that, in later years.

Despite the hilly nature of much of the county, Shropshire was covered with airfields during the Second World War. They were so close together that it was sometimes possible for a pilot in trouble on take-off to land straight ahead at a different airfield! The county, being on the Eastern side of England was seen as the ideal site for many training airfields.

Most of these airfields had satellite fields attached to them, either as relief landing grounds for Maintenance Units which operated from Cosford, Shawbury and Tern Hillfor training units, or as extra storage space.

Some of these minor airfields, often little more than a grass field, with the minimal amount of accommodation, are illustrated in the following section, though one, Bridleway Gate, has defied all attempts by the authors to find any kind of illustration.

There were even more basic airfields than the SLGs and RLGs, for instance the 'Piper Cub' strips used by most US Army units, and the strip attached to the RAF radio station at Buntingsdale Hall, near Tern Hill, used by communications Lysanders.

In more recent years the microlight movement has created a number of airfields, not dissimilar to those wartime SLGs, or even the fields used by Hucks and Hamel before 1914. These too are illustrated here.

B.C. Hucks at the controls of his Bleriot Monoplane in 1912 during his aerial tour of the country. He was to repeat the tour in 1913, by which time he had become the first British pilot to loop the loop. He operated from a number of fields in Shropshire during both tours, including Ludford Park, Ludlow, where the Cattle Market now is. In 1913 he demonstrated his loop at each venue and gave rides at ten shillings a time.

Naval aviators relaxing on the side of an air raid shelter at RAF Bratton in 1943. Used as a Relief Landing Ground for several airfields, including Hinstock, Bratton, just north of Wellington, was just a grass airfield with very few permanent buildings, like so many RLGs.

The Watch Office at RAF Condover, south of Shrewsbury in 1979, with 'Flying Control' still visible above the upper windows. The building alongside is a Floodlight Trailer and Tractor shed. A large substantial airfield, with three concrete runways, a T1 and nine blister hangars, RAF Condover was used as a satellite of Shawbury, and then Tern Hill until it closed in 1945.

The entire personnel at RAF Brockton, a Satellite Landing Ground at Sutton Maddock, between Shifnal and Bridgnorth. Arguably, Brockton is Shropshire's oldest airfield as James Valentine landed his Bleriot Monoplane there during an air race on 31 July 1911. Used for storing aircraft from No.9 MU, Cosford during the Second World War, it soon reverted to agriculture, but is now occasionally used by the microlights of the Shropshire Aero Club, from nearby Shifnal – meaning it has been used as an airfield for nearly ninety years!

The Aerodrome Control in 1976 at RAF Chetwynd, which is a Relief Landing Ground with greater survival instincts than most. Built as an RLG for the Masters of No.5(P) AFU at Tern Hill, it was never more than a grass field. It continued in use after the war, used by 6 FTS, and then by the helicopters from Shawbury.

The new airfield control building at RAF Chetwynd. This is now used by the Defence Helicopter Flying School from Shawbury and, occasionally, by Lockheed Hercules transports bringing in SAS troops on training missions.

A Robin hangar at RAF Weston Park, disguised at a gamekeeper's cottage. Another SLG used by No.9 MU at Cosford for storing aircraft, this grass airfield lay on the Shropshire part of the estate.

A Gazelle helicopter from RAF Shawbury at a Weston Park Air Day in 1986. The Air Day took place on the Staffordshire part of the estate, not on the former Second World War airfield.

The staff at RAF Hodnet during the war, in front of one of their charges, a Lockheed Hudson. Yet another SLG which had three 'parents' after its opening in June 1941. Firstly it stored aircraft from No.27 MU, Tern Hill, then No.37 MU, Burtonwood, and finally No.27 MU, Shawbury. The landing area was south of the A53 with most of the aircraft stored in the grounds of Hodnet Hall, on the other side of the road. One small building is still in use as Hodnet's cricket pavilion! Third from the right in the front row is Corporal Arthur Braithwaite, in charge of Transport.

In August 1978 some of the former surviving RAF buildings at Bratton RLG were in use by Long Lane farm. The single brick wall construction is evident of this temporary building of a type seen on many airfields. Bratton had a number of blister hangars and land south of the airfield is now covered by new housing.

A flex-wing microlight of the Shropshire Aero Club, on their airfield at Haughton Hall Farm, near Shifnal. Shropshire's newest airfield, Shifnal was opened in 1997, against fierce planning opposition.

One of the privately owned microlights at Shifnal, a Noble Hardman Snowbird Mk.IV, G-MVIO, shows how far modern lightweight materials have enabled manufacturers to build 'microlights' just like normal three-axes light aircraft.

A Vickers Vimy being overhauled inside one of the two Belfast Truss hangars at Monkmoor, near Shrewsbury. A field next to Monkmoor racecourse had been used by Gustav Hamler in 1912 and, in 1918, an airfield was opened at Monkmoor as home for the Observer's School of Reconnaissance & Aerial Photography, with twenty-four aircraft. However, it is not known if this Vimy was one of those. The unit was disbanded on 2 May 1919.

Avro 504Ks of Berkshire Aviation Tours at Monkmoor on 15 May 1929, including G-EBOB Berkshire were a well-known joy-riding company formed in 1921 and, in the winter of 1928-1929, used Monkmoor as a base. In May 1929 they amalgamated with Noirthern Airlines to form Northern Air Transport Ltd with sixteen Avro 504s on strength.

A modern side view of the twin-shed First-World-War Belfast Truss hangar. One roof has now been replaced by a pitched roof. Now in use as part of an industrial estate, the hangar had housed No.34 MU during the Second World War, salvaging crashed aircraft.

One of the additional buildings erected during the Second World War for the use of No.34 MU probably as an office. Beacause of the expansion of Shrewsbury, there was no airfield at Monkmoor during the Second World War.

The Watch Office at RAF Montford Bridge. The original building is to the left, a typical building, type 17658/40, for a fighter satellite station, Rednal being the parent station. The two-storey extension was later built to provide a better view. In the case of Condover a new tower was built. Used almost totally by the Spitfires of No.61 OTU, Montford Bridge reverted to agriculture after the war. This forlorn tower is now typical of many such silent sentinels scattered across Shropshire, reminders of wartime days when the skies above the county were filled with aircraft.

Acknowledgements

So many people have been helpful in the compilation of this book, but the authors are particularly grateful to Toby Neal of the Shropshire Star, for access to many contributors, via his occasional series on Shropshire airfields and the help he provided.

We also wish to thank the editors of the sister newspapers, the *Bridgnorth Journal*, the Newport Advertiser and the *Shrewsbury Chronicle*. Among the contacts these led to were Ron Howard of Eaton Constantine and his marvellous pictures of RNAS Hinstock, Dave Williams, who operates part of Peplow, Major Ervin Miller, and his irreplaceable photographs of Atcham.

For photographs of Shawbury, the authors are grateful to Sqd. Ldr Martin Locke, CRO, RAF Shawbury. For many of the wartime pictures we are grateful to Andy Thomas for letting us draw on his large collection.

Others who provided pictures, information or assistance are David Adams, Peter Broom, Alf Evans, Aldon Ferguson, Roger Freeman, R.R. Glass, James J. Halley, Terry Holden, Les Jones, Dennis Moore, Richard Neal, George Preece, Brian Robinson, H.D. Rylands, Andy Simpson, David Smith, R.C. Sturtivant, Don Thompson, Dave Welch, Jim Wilson, John Francis and the RAF Museum at Cosford. Also the Midland Gliding Club.